Two Lovely Misses

MER GIRL

THE
SPORTSWOMAN
DAYBOOK

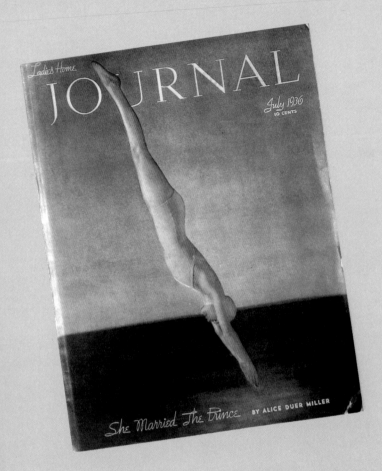

Ladies Home

JOURNAL

July 1936
10 CENTS

She Married The Prince BY ALICE DUER MILLER

THE
SPORTSWOMAN DAYBOOK

 ERNESTINE G. MILLER

Harry N. Abrams, Inc., Publishers

This book is dedicated to my mother and father, Gertrude and Lawrence Gichner, and to my daughter, Helene Stephanie Miller.

EDITOR: Ruth Peltason
DESIGNER: Dana Sloan
PHOTOGRAPHY: John Parnell

The magazine covers featured in this book are from the collection of Ernestine Miller

The Publisher wishes to thank Walter Reed for his kind help and cooperation

The Saturday Evening Post © The Curtis Publishing Company

The magazine covers on pages 2, 13, 19, 43, 63, 75, 83, and 99 are reprinted from *Ladies' Home Journal,* 1901, 1904, 1907, 1911, 1912, 1931, 1934, 1936

Printed and bound in Hong Kong

INTRODUCTION

S ports have increasingly become a part of a woman's daily life, whether for the sheer benefit of exercise, the pleasure of recreation, or for the purpose of athletic competition. Although it has taken years—decades, really— for women to be widely recognized and accepted as athletes, women have been active in sports for centuries.

Through a fascinating array of magazine cover illustration, *The Sportswoman Daybook* chronicles the sports culture of women during the early decades of the twentieth century. These images are a colorful visual record of the customs and fashions of the day, and they also show the important role that magazines played in a woman's life.

Before the advent of radio and television, the monthly magazine was a much-anticipated arrival. Serving as a main source of information, the magazine kept readers informed on politics and important news items of the day; soon, the leading magazines also included serious journalism, poetry, and literary fiction. For women especially, the magazine offered advice on the home and children, employment and education, decoration and fashion, and above all, it connected women with each other.

The most successful of these women's magazines—*The Ladies' Home Journal, Good Housekeeping, Redbook, Woman's Home Companion*—in addition to giving advice on marriage and child-rearing also portrayed the American sportswoman. As seen on numerous magazine covers, sometimes this figure of athleticism was one of the country-club set, but just as often she was an average young woman glowing with health and vigor, proof that any woman could engage in sports. And the variety of sports for women was, and still is, wide: tennis, golf, skiing, skating, basketball, fencing, fishing, canoeing, swimming, bicycling.

The ideal American sportswoman was created by illustrators whose names rank as leaders in their field: Maxfield Parrish, Howard Chandler Christy, Coles Phillips, Edward Penfield, Arthur Dove. These "image makers" have left behind a legacy that is rich for its visual appeal as well as its portrayal of a time in history. Today, the magazine covers by these illustrators are eagerly sought by collectors, who admire their artistic beauty and charm. This popular art form is a contribution to the broader appreciation and encouragement of women's participation in sports.

Ernestine Gichner Miller

JANUARY

1

New Year's Day

2

3

4

5

6

The first American figure
skating tournament was in
1914; Theresa Weld of
Massachusetts won the
ladies' singles.

7

THE·YOUTH'S·COMPANION

Albert D Stelle

217 F. Market St

Jan11

NEW·YEAR'S·NUMBER·1911

JANUARY

8

9

10

11

12

13

Overland trekking on
snowshoes eventually lost
out in popularity to cross-
country skiing.

14

January

20 Cents

Cosmopolitan

A "Penrod"
Serial
By
Booth
Tarkington
PENROD
JASHBER
(His career as
a Detective)
Begins in
this issue

JANUARY

15

16

17

18

19

20

21

Alpine—or downhill—skiing
was given Olympic recognition
in 1936.

JANUARY, 1931
Volume XLVIII, Number 1

10 Cents
By subscription $1.00.
In the United States
and in Canada.

LADIES' HOME
JOURNAL

Beginning TAXI: a Vivid New Serial by ALICE DUER MILLER
Also Sophie Kerr—Norman Bel Geddes—Konrad Bercovici—W. B. Seabrook

JANUARY

22

23

24

25

26

27

The steel skate blade was
developed in the U.S. in 1850;
this refinement led to the huge
boom in figure skating.

28

THE PEOPLE'S HOME JOURNAL

JANUARY 1912

FIVE CENTS

F. M. LUPTON, Publisher. NEW YORK

January ❦ February

29

30

31

1

2

3

4

At the age of 21, in 1956, Tenley Albright became the first American woman to win the Olympic gold medal in figure skating.

FEBRUARY 1907

15 CENTS

GOOD
HOUSEKEEPING

THE PHELPS PUBLISHING CO. Springfield, Mass.

February

5

6

7

8

9

10

11

America's first winter
playground for the rich and
famous was Sun Valley, Idaho,
which opened in 1936.

LADIES' HOME
JOURNAL

10 c.
CANADA
12 CENTS

FEBRUARY, 1934

VOLUME LI
NUMBER 2

NRA
WE DO OUR PART

ALICE ROOSEVELT LONGWORTH · ALICE DUER MILLER · FANNY HEASLIP LEA
PAUL DE KRUIF · THE LORIMERS · EDITH WHARTON · FRANCES NOYES HART

FEBRUARY

12

Lincoln's Birthday

13

14

Valentine's Day

15

16

17

Fencing requires the player
to touch the opponent's torso
with the weapon, while
avoiding attack.

18

THE SATURDAY EVENING POST
An Illustrated Weekly
Founded
by Benj. Franklin
10c. in Canada
APRIL 1, 1933
5cts. THE COPY
THOMAS McMORROW · GEORGE WESTON · MARK SULLIVAN

FEBRUARY

19

20

21

22

Washington's Birthday

23

24

New Hampshire was the site of the first ski school, which opened in 1929. Three years later the first winter Olympics in the U.S. took place at Lake Placid, New York.

25

THE CROWELL PUBLISHING COMPANY

The February American Magazine

25 Cents

Haskell Coffin

LINCOLN—The Most Lied About Man
By Honoré Willsie Morrow

February 1928

THE AMERICAN MAGAZINE

FEBRUARY ❄ MARCH

26

27

28

29

1

2

3

Women's ski attire traditionally consisted of long wool skirts for the sake of propriety. By the 1930s, however, more sensible clothing had been designed.

MARCH 1907   TEN CENTS

WOMAN'S HOME COMPANION

The
Crowell
Publishing
Company.

MARCH

4

5

6

7

8

9

10

Billie Jean King single-handedly changed the course of women's tennis: her greatness on the court was matched by aggressive lobbying for better prize money and the expansion of the pro circuit for women.

5¢ a copy

July 29, 1916

Collier's

THE NATIONAL WEEKLY

EAGLE SHANNON ROPES ONE by Richard Washburn Child

MARCH

11

12

13

14

15

16

Stanford University and the
University of California,
Berkeley, dueled in the first
women's college basketball
game in 1896.

17

St. Patrick's Day

Four Dollars a Year   New York, December 19th, 1903   Ten Cents a Copy

THE ILLVSTRATED
SPORTING NEWS

With Department devoted to the Drama

Volume II   Number 32

MARCH

18

19

20

21

22

23

Of all gymnastic events, the
rings demand the greatest
upper body strength.

24

May 14, 1932

Collier's

THE NATIONAL WEEKLY ★

5¢ a copy
10c in
Canada

JOSEPH
FARRELLY

**Octavus Roy Cohen ~ Sax Rohmer ~ Alan Le May
Elmer Davis ~ Owen P. White ~ Clinton W. Gilbert**

MARCH

25

26

27

28

29

30

From the time of her debut at
the age of 17 in 1935 through
1940, Patty Berg won every
important American title
in women's golf.

31

HARPER'S BAZAR

MARCH 1910

APRIL

1

April Fool's Day

2

3

4

5

6

The best trout fishing waters
are clustered in and around
Michigan, Montana, and
Idaho, although equally great
rivers, streams, and brooks
7 abound in Arkansas, New
York, Pennsylvania, New
Hampshire, Vermont,
Colorado, and Arizona.

NO. 2535　　　　　　APRIL 7, 1904　　　　　　PRICE 10 CENTS

LESLIE'S WEEKLY

THE TROUT-FISHING SEASON OPENS

Drawn for *Leslie's Weekly* by Gifford Ryder

APRIL

8

9

10

11

12

13

No matter how hard she pedaled or how far she swam, magazines showed the young American girl as a picture of health: smiling, rosy-cheeked, and always full of energy.

14

THE SATURDAY EVENING POST

An Illustrated Weekly
Founded A. D. 1728 by Benj. Franklin

APRIL 28, 1934

Volume 206, Number 44

5 cts. THE COPY

10c. in Canada
(INCLUDING TAX)

THOMAS McMORROW · HAROLD TITUS · J. P. MARQUAND

APRIL

15

16

17

18

19

20

For the upper-class Victorian
young woman, fencing offered
an acceptable means for
releasing aggression.

21

VOL. LVI, NO. 1453
COPYRIGHT, 1910, BY
LIFE PUBLISHING CO.

SPORTSMAN'S NUMBER

PRICE, 10 CENTS
SEPTEMBER 1, 1910

LIFE

C COLES PHILLIPS

April

22

23

24

25

26

27 A fully-fitted leather glove was
meant to protect the lady
golfer's fine hands.

28

THE SATURDAY EVENING POST

An Il— Weekly
Foun—led — enj. Franklin

10c. in Canada
(INCLUDING TAX)

Volume 205, Number 43

APRIL 22, 1933

5cts. THE COPY

PEARL BUCK · GUY GILPATRIC · WALTER D. EDMONDS.

APRIL ❦ MAY

29

30

1

2

3

4

Women who played the
baseline game of tennis's early
days were outfitted in long
sleeves and voluminous skirts.

5

THE SUMMER
FASHION NUMBER

THE
LADIES'
HOME
JOURNAL

Painted by Henry Hutt

JUNE 1907   THE CURTIS PUBLISHING COMPANY, PHILADELPHIA   FIFTEEN CENTS

Copyright, 1907 (Trade-Mark Registered), by The Curtis Publishing Company, in the United States and Great Britain. London, 5, Henrietta Street, Covent Garden, W. C.

MAY

6

7

8

9

10

11

Crew for women was first
introduced in 1875 at
Wellesley College.

12

Vol. XV - No. 482   New York, July 11th 1896.   Price Ten Cents.

TRUTH

Jay Hambidge

HARVARD AND YALE, BEWARE!

ERE LONG THE VASSAR AND THE WELLESLEY CREWS
MAY WIN THE PENNANT FROM THE "REDS" AND "BLUES."

MAY

13

14

15

16

17

18

Few outdoor sports caught on as quickly as did golf, which was first played in America in 1888 and soon became synonymous with the good life.

19

Vol. XXI.   MAY, 1899.   No. 2.

THE MUNSEY

FRANK A. MUNSEY, PUBLISHER, 111 FIFTH AVENUE, NEW YORK.

MAY

20

21

22

23

24

25

The Newport casino, with its
celebrated grass courts, opened
in 1880 and is today the site
of the International Tennis Hall
of Fame.

26

THE SATURDAY EVENING POST
NRA CODE
Founded
Benj. Franklin
JUNE 16, 1934
5cts. THE COPY
10c. in Canada
GARET GARRETT · GEORGE BRADSHAW · SAM HELLMAN

MAY ❦ JUNE

27

28

29

30

31

1

2

THE SATURDAY EVENING POST

An Illustrated Weekly
Founded A° D. 1728 by Benj. Franklin

Vol. 192, No. 52. Published Weekly at Philadelphia. Entered as Second-Class Matter, November 18, 1879, at the Post Office at Philadelphia, Under the Act of March 3, 1879.

JUNE 26, 1920

5c. THE COPY
10c. in Canada

DRAWN BY
CLARENCE F. UNDERWOOD

Beginning: STEEL—By JOSEPH HERGESHEIMER

JUNE

3

4

5

6

7

8

In 1891 the Shinnecock Hills
Golf Club opened in
Southampton, New York;
within 2 years a separate
course for women—the first of
its kind—was created.

9

THE SATURDAY EVENING POST

An Illus...........ly
Founded A° D: .... J. Franklin

Volume 200. Number 50

5c THE COPY
10c. In Canada

**Alice Duer Miller—Joseph Hergesheimer—Don Marquis—James Warner Bellah
Struthers Burt—Elizabeth Frazer—W. O. McGeehan—Richard Washburn Child**

JUNE

10

11

12

13

14

Flag Day

15

In the 1920s Helen Wills
ushered in a new kind of
tennis: competitive, focused,
and daring.

16

JULY 1932

THIRTY. CENTS IN CANADA

The American Magazine

25¢

Complete
in this Issue

A Mystery
Story By

DASHIELL
HAMMETT

Sheridan

How to Make a Job for Y

© THE CROWELL PUBLISHING COMPANY

JUNE

17

18

19

20

21

22

Pat McCormick was the U.S.
diving champion in the 1950s.
In the 1952 Olympics in
Helsinki, McCormick won
both the springboard and
platform events. Her
daughter competed in the
1984 Olympics.

23

JUDGE

JUNE 26, 1926 ★

PRICE 15 CENTS

"WELL I SWAN!"

JUNE

24

25

26

27

28

29

One of the great promoters of women's golf in its infancy was Mildred "Babe" Didrickson Zaharias, a former Olympic champion, renowned for her showy style and numerous championships.

30

Collier's

THE NATIONAL WEEKLY

The First Tee

VOL XLIX NO 17

JUNE 8 1912

JULY

1

2

3

4

Independence Day

5

6

7

The Victorians considered
sports too strenuous for a
young girl at puberty; today, a
15-year-old can turn pro and
compete at the highest levels of
women's tennis.

THE YOUTH'S COMPANION

INDEPENDENCE NUMBER 1916

JULY

8

9

10

11

12

13

In 1926, Gertrud Ederle, already an Olympic champion with 18 world records, became the first woman to swim across the English Channel. Her record time of 14 hours, 31 minutes, beat the 5 previous male swimmers by roughly 2 hours.

14

THE ALL-STORY NUMBER

THE LADIES' HOME JOURNAL

PAINTED BY C. COLES PHILLIPS

JULY, 1911

FIFTEEN CENTS

THE CURTIS PUBLISHING COMPANY, PHILADELPHIA

JULY

15

16

17

18

19

20

21

In 1874 the new game of lawn
tennis was introduced in the
U.S. by Mary Outerbridge,
who played with her brothers
in Staten Island, New York.

Vol. XX

THE DESIGNER

for July

C. Kleinschmidt

80 Cents a Year
Post-paid

Standard Fashion Company

10 Cents a Copy

12-16 Vandam Street New York

33 Richmond Street West, Toronto, Canada

Entered at the Post Office, New York, as Second-Class Mail Matter

JULY

22

23

24

25

26

27

28

PICTORIAL
REVIEW

A NEW SERIAL
BY
ELEANOR
HALLOWELL
ABBOTT
IN THIS ISSUE

JULY 1915
FIFTEEN CENTS

THE PICTORIAL REVIEW COMPANY, NEW YORK

JULY ❦ AUGUST

29

30

31

1

2

3

4

Eventually the competitive
edge won out in women's
tennis: rolled-up sleeves and
a strong net game became
increasingly commonplace.

THE SUNDAY
MAGAZINE

NEW-YORK, JULY 17, 1904.   New-York Tribune.   PART III

The Court Favorite.

AUGUST

5

6

7

8

9

USTA team playdayears.
I gave it all on Sat 10th
but couldn't do it on
Sun.
a learning exp.

10

11

On September 1, 1910, Nan
Jane Aspinwall galloped out of
San Francisco on the way to
being the first woman to cross
the country on horseback.
She arrived in Manhattan 301
days later (108 of them actual
travel days).

Midsummer Story Number

WOMAN'S HOME COMPANION

AUGUST 1913   FIFTEEN CENTS

THE CROWELL PUBLISHING COMPANY

W. HERBERT DUNTON

AUGUST

12

13

14

15

16

17

18

The graceful swan dive, similar to the straightforward platform dive, looks easy but is difficult to perform perfectly.

Life

AUGUST 4, 1921

PRICE 15 CENTS

COLES PHILLIPS

For Divers Reasons

AUGUST

19

20

21

22

23

24

The shift from calisthenics to
sports was first developed for
girls and young women at the
school and university levels.

25

THE LADIES' HOME JOURNAL

AUGUST 1912

FIFTEEN CENTS

PAINTED BY
HARRISON FISHER

THE CURTIS PUBLISHING COMPANY PHILADELPHIA

Copyright, 1912 (Trade Mark Registered) by The Curtis Publishing Company, in the United States and Great Britain. London: G. Newnes Limited, Covent Garden, W. C.

26

27

28

29

30

31

Diving, readily linked to aerial
gymnastics, combines grace
with stunning twists, rotations,
and somersaults.

1

Life

August 4 1927
Price 15 cents

SEPTEMBER

2

3

4

5

6

7

8

The turn-of-the-century belief
held that the "education of a
young woman's limbs"—no
matter how much fun—was not
to replace her main function: as
wife and caretaker of the home.

THE SATURDAY EVENING POST
An Illustrated Weekly
AUG.19,'16
5c. THE COPY
DRAWN BY CLARENCE F. UNDERWOOD
GULLIBLE'S TRAVELS—By Ring W. Lardner

SEPTEMBER

9

10

11

12

13

14

15

Eleonora Sears, a Boston
Brahmin related to Thomas
Jefferson, was considered
daring by playing polo in
jodhpurs in the early 1900s.

SEPTEMBER

16

17

18

19

20

21

Corseted waistlines and ankle-
length skirts may have looked
attractive, but they only
hindered the serious player.

22

THE LADIES' HOME JOURNAL

FOR NOVEMBER 1901

Thomas
Mitchell
Peirce

TEN CENTS

THE CURTIS PUBLISHING COMPANY, PHILADELPHIA

SEPTEMBER

23

24

25

26

27

28

The United States Open has
been played at three venues in
its history: Newport, Rhode
Island, 1881–1914; Forest
Hills, New York, 1915–1977;
Flushing Meadows, New York,
1978–present.

29

THE SATURDAY EVENING POST

An Illustrated Weekly
Founded ~~~~~~ Benj. Franklin

NOV. 9, 1912   **5cts. THE COPY**

"DRAWN BY
CLARENCE F. UNDERWOOD

MORE THAN 1,900,000 CIRCULATION WEEKLY

SEPTEMBER ❦ OCTOBER

30

1

2

3

4

5

6

In May 1932, the first
international women's golf
match, the Curtis Cup, took
place between the United
States and Great Britain.

October 8, 1917

Every Week

$1⁰⁰ a Year

3¢

COPYRIGHT, 1917, BY THE CROWELL PUBLISHING CO.

Thomas Fink

OCTOBER

7

8

9

10

11

12

Columbus Day

Sidesaddle was for many years
the acceptable riding style for a
woman, although in fact it was
a highly dangerous mount for
any considerable riding.

13

WIDOWS' NUMBER

Life

PRICE 10 CENTS
Vol. 60, No. 1574 December 26, 1912
Copyright, 1912, Life Publishing Company

COLES PHILLIPS

CLASS I. WIDOWS

OCTOBER

14

15

16

17

18

19

In 1953, the U.S. Women's
Open became part of the
national championships
organized by the USGA.

20

N. S. K.

Modern Priscilla

Needlework — Fashions — Fiction — Housekeeping

The
Magazine
That Helps

October
1922
Twenty
Cents

OCTOBER

21

22

23

24

25

26

27

Whether riding in the East or in the Midwest, the traditional costume for the well-groomed equestrian was relatively unchanged, from hat to crop.

OCTOBER ❖ NOVEMBER

28

29

30

31

Halloween

1

2

In 1949, 11 top female
players established the
Ladies Professional Golf
Association (LPGA).

3

25 Cents

October 1927

The RED BOOK

MAGAZINE

Something New
in Stories of Today by

Rupert Hughes

Sam Hellman
Frank R. Adams
Margaret Culkin
Banning
and
Others

OCTOBER 1927   THE RED BOOK MAGAZINE   Vol. 49 No. 6

NOVEMBER

4

5

6

7

8

9

10

The first women's basketball
team was organized in 1892 at
Smith College in Northampton,
Massachusetts.

THE SATURDAY EVENING POST

An Illustrated Weekly Magazine
Founded ~~A~~ by Benj. Franklin

NOV. 20, 1909   5cts. THE COPY

Carol Aus

More Than a Million and a Quarter Circulation Weekly

November

11

12

13

14

15

16

17

In luxury communities, such as
Tuxedo Park in New York, the
affluent sportswoman could
indulge herself daily in the
pleasures of riding.

THE MAGAZINE WITH A MILLION

THE LADIES' HOME JOURNAL

NOVEMBER 1904   TEN CENTS

THE CURTIS PUBLISHING COMPANY, PHILADELPHIA

November

18

19

20

21

22

23

24

The first National Women's
Basketball Championship was
played in Los Angeles in 1926.

Pictorial Review

November

1911

Fifteen Cents

NOVEMBER ❧ DECEMBER

25

26

27

28

29

30

1

Figure skaters train hard but
make the form look easy. This
was especially true of Olympic
champion Peggy Fleming,
whose delicacy belied her
strength and stamina.

GOOD HOUSEKEEPING

JANUARY, 1917

15 CENTS

COLES PHILLIPS

DECEMBER

2

3

4

5

6

7

8

In a Canadian newspaper
account of 1875 the term "ice
hockey" was first used; it
described a game played at
Victoria Skating Rink
in Montreal.

THE SUNDAY MAGAZINE

New-York Tribune.

NEW-YORK,
JANUARY 15, 1905

PART III

The Hockey Girl - "Coaxing"

H.V.PARKHURST

DECEMBER

9

10

11

12

13

14

15

The National Ski Association
was formed in 1904. Today,
between 6 and 7 million skiers
take to the slopes annually
in the U.S.

Modern Priscilla

February 1922

Twenty Cents and Worth More

Marguerite Davis

DECEMBER

16

17

18

19

20

21

Snowshoe cross-country races,
obstacle races, and hikes were a
popular sport of colleges
located in the snowbelt regions.

22

THE SATURDAY EVENING POST

An Illust
Founded A⁰ D⁰ 17

Volume 201, Number 30

JAN. 26, '29

10c. in Canada

5c.

Haskell Coffin

Day Edgar—Howard Mingos—Isaac F. Marcosson—Arthur William Brown
Nina Wilcox Putnam—Mary F. Watkins—Samuel G. Blythe—Booth Jameson

DECEMBER

23

24

Christmas Eve

25

Christmas Day

26

Boxing Day (Canada)

27

28

Norwegian Olympic champion Sonia Henie, later a movie star, has been described as a "Degas ballerina" on the ice. From her first appearance in the U.S. in 1936, her competitive edge and charm helped popularize figure skating.

29

December

30

31

New Year's Eve

Although downhill skiing has always been a relatively social sport, cross-country on snowshoes allowed for more solitary appreciation of the outdoors.

THE·YOUTH'S·COMPANION

NEW·YEAR'S
NUMBER
1915

BIOGRAPHIES of ILLUSTRATORS

Carol Aus (1868–1934)

Aus was born in Norway and studied at the Academie Julian in Paris. She later moved to Chicago, where she lived for the rest of her life.

Howard Chandler Christy (1873–1960)

Christy first became known as a writer and illustrator of military stories for the literary magazines *Harper's*, *Scribners*, and *Leslie's*, as well as for the posters he drew for the Navy, the Marines, and the American Red Cross. His famous "Christy Girl," the subject for most of his work, represented the ideal American woman — elegant, spirited, and beautiful. Early in his career Christy achieved fame. President Calvin Coolidge commissioned him to paint his portrait, yet perhaps Christy's greatest accomplishment was a 20-by-30-foot canvas he made for the Capitol Building in Washington, D.C. The work, titled *The Signing of the Constitution*, still hangs in the grand stairway there.

Haskell Coffin (1878–1941)

Coffin was born in New York City and studied at the Corcoran School of Art in Washington, D.C., as well as in Paris. His illustrations were commissioned by the popular *American Magazine* in the 1920s and 1930s.

Marguerite Davis (1889–?)

Davis knew early on that she wanted to be an illustrator — by the age of five she had begun to draw and seemingly never stopped. Davis, who was born in Quincy, Massachusetts, attended Vassar College and studied at the Museum of Fine Art in Boston. Davis was best known as an illustrator of children's books.

Arthur Garfield Dove (1880–1946)

Dove was born in Geneva, New York, and as a child was taught to draw and paint by his neighbor, himself an amateur painter. Dove attended Hobart College and later transferred to Cornell University, where he made illustrations for the yearbook. Although today he is most famous as a painter, Dove began in advertising in New York and later worked as a free-lance artist. Dove's illustrations appeared in numerous popular magazines, among them *McClure's Magazine, Century, Collier's,* and *The Illustrated Sporting News.* In 1920 he moved onto a boat on Long Island Sound and spent the next ten years doing humorous illustrations—often for children's stories.

William Herbert "Buck" Dunton (1878–1936)

Dunton was born in Augusta, Maine, and studied at Cowles Art School and the Art Students League of Boston. Dunton became famous for illustrations and paintings of the West. He set up a studio in Taos, New Mexico, in 1912 and became a resident there in 1921.

Denman Fink (1880–1956)

A native of Pennsylvania, Fink studied at the Pittsburgh School of Design. His illustrations were published by *Harper's, Scribner's, Century,* and *The Saturday Evening Post.*

Harrison Fisher (1875–1934)

Fisher was born in Brooklyn, New York, and at the age of six moved with his family to San Francisco. His early training came from his father, Hugh Antoine Fisher, a landscape painter, although he received formal training at the Mark Hopkins Institute of Art. Fisher first received recognition for his sketches in the San Francisco newspapers. He returned to New York City and was hired by *Puck* magazine, where his talent for drawing beautiful women was established. His Fisher "Body Girl" was his trademark for years and rivaled the drawings of young women by Charles Dana Gibson and Howard Chandler Christy. For many years Fisher had an exclusive contract with *Cosmopolitan Magazine.* In later life he worked as a portrait painter.

Jay Hambidge (1867–1924)

Hambidge was born in Canada and studied at the Art Students League in New York. He worked as an illustrator for most of his life.

Guy Hoff (1889–1962)

Hoff was born in Rochester, New York, and received formal training at the Art School of the Albright Gallery in Buffalo and at the Art Students League in New York City.

In New York Hoff illustrated program covers for the Shubert Theatres; however, it was the sale of his first cover to the magazine *Smart Set* that brought him national attention. He also illustrated covers for *The Saturday Evening Post* and *Pictorial Review*, among others, and created advertisements for Procter & Gamble, Lux, and Ivory soap.

John Newton Howitt (1885–1958)

Newton attended the Art Students League, and was an illustrator of cover designs for national magazines and advertising posters.

Henry Hutt (1875–1950)

Hutt was born in Chicago and studied at the Art Institute there. He sold his first picture to the original *Life* magazine at the age of sixteen and thereafter illustrated for most of the leading American magazines of the day.

Arthur Ignatius Keller (1866–1924)

Keller was trained at the National Academy of Design, and his drawings show great technical mastery.

John La Gatta (1894–1977)

La Gatta was born in Naples, Italy, but was educated in the United States at the New York School of Fine and Applied Arts. His first jobs were in advertising, but over time his work was in demand by major magazines. La Gatta spent the later years of his life in Los Angeles, teaching at the Art Center School. He was elected to the Society of Illustrators Hall of Fame in 1984.

Cushman Parker (1881–1940)

Parker was born in Boston, Massachusetts. He was a member of the Society of Illustrators, and designed covers for various magazines, among them *Saturday*

Evening Post, *McCall's*, and *Collier's*. However, he was perhaps best known for the work he did for the Bon Ami conmpany, with whom he was affiliated for many years.

Maxfield Parrish (1870–1953)
Parrish's reputation today soars well beyond the world of magazine illustration. His painter father, Stephen Parrish, taught his son the basics of painting at the age of three. Parrish attended Haverford College, where art and classical architecture were his main areas of interest; his love for architecture influenced his style of painting throughout his life. After college Parrish attended the Pennsylvania Academy of Fine Art. His first commissioned work was for the cover of *Harper's Bazaar* in 1895. Fame followed soon thereafter. In 1898 Parrish moved to Cornish, New Hampshire, where he lived for the rest of his life. From 1903 to 1910 he had an exclusive contract with *Collier's* to make the artwork for their covers. Blessed with a diversity of talents, the artist was typically recognized by the now-classic "Parrish blue." Parrish's prodigious output included paintings, illustrated books, murals, and advertising graphics.

Edward Penfield (1866–1925)
Penfield was born in Brooklyn, New York, and studied at the Art Students League. He was the art editor at *Harper's* magazine from 1890 to 1901. He also illustrated covers for *Collier's* magazine. Penfield's easily recognizable style of large flat shapes, clean lines, and minimal detail greatly influenced American illustration. Penfield was a pioneer in bringing French and Japanese influence to bear on American poster design.

Coles Phillips (1880–1927)
Phillips was born in Springfield, Ohio, and attended Kenyon College; there he made illustrations for the school magazine. After college he moved to New York, where he first worked in advertising and later opened his own studio for artists. Coles's famous "Fadeaway Girl" was first published as a color cover for *Life* magazine. His fadeaway technique tied the picture into the background either by color or pattern and the careful planning of shapes, creating a posterlike effect.

John Sheridan (1880–1948)

Sheridan was born in the Midwest, in Wisconsin, and attended Georgetown University, in Washington, D.C. At one time in his career he was art editor of the *Washington Evening Star*, and later helped to produce the all-color insert for the *San Francisco Chronicle*. Sheridan's art was seen on the covers of *The Ladies' Home Journal*, *The Saturday Evening Post*, and *The American Magazine*.

Penrhyn Stanlaws (1877–1957)

Stanlaws is noted for his drawings of very attractive young women, whose faces graced the covers of such magazines as *The Saturday Evening Post*, *Associated Sunday Magazine*, and *Hearst's International*.

Clarence Underwood (1871–1929)

Underwood was born in New York and studied at the Art Students League there and at the Academie Julian in Paris. His illustrations were commissioned for *Century*, *McClure's*, *Harper's*, and *The Saturday Evening Post*. The women in his illustrations were described as having a "wholesome Americanism," evoking great feeling and sense of the outdoors.

Charles D. Williams (1875–1954)

Williams, who at one time in his career worked as a professional lightweight boxer, was actively involved with the Society of Illustrators.

INDEX of ILLUSTRATORS

Arthur I. Keller—week of May 13–19

C. Kleinschmidt—week of July 15–21

John La Gatta—weeks of February 5–11; August 26–September 1

F. Miller—week of July 22–28

Cushman Parker—week of January 29–February 4

H.L.V. Parkhurst—weeks of March 25–31; December 2–8

Maxfield Parrish—week of January 15–21

Thomas Mitchell Peirce—week of September 16–22

Edward Penfield—weeks of March 4–10; June 24–30; October 21–27

Coles Phillips—weeks of April 15–21; July 8–14; August 12–18;
September 9–15; October 7–13; November 25–December 1

Gifford Ryder—week of April 1–7

Valentine Sandberg—week of December 23–29

John Sheridan—week of June 10–16

Penrhyn Stanlaws—weeks of April 22–28; May 20–26; June 3–9

W. D. Stevens—weeks of January 1–7; July 1–7

Clarence Underwood—weeks of May 27–June 2; June 3–9;
September 2–8; September 23–29

Charles D. Williams—week of January 22–28

Play Ball

Serves you right

T. EARL CHRISTY

THE PILOT